Adoniram Judson

God's Man in Burma

Sharon Hambrick

journeyforth®

Greenville, South Carolina

Library of Congress Cataloging-in-Publication Data

Hambrick, Sharon, 1961-
    Adoniram Judson : God's Man in Burma / Sharon Hambrick.
        p. cm.
Summary: Presents the life of the early nineteenth-century missionary
who endured many hardships working and teaching in Burma and
translated the Bible into Burmese.
        ISBN 1-57924-625-7 (perfect bound : alk. paper)
        [1. Judson, Adoniram, 1788-1850—Juvenile literature.
2. Missionaries—Burma—Biography—Juvenile literature.
3. Missionaries—United States—Biography—Juvenile literature.
[1. Judson, Adoniram, 1788-1850. 2. Missionaries.] I. Title.

        BV3271.J7 H36 2001
        266'.61'092—dc21   2001002829

Adoniram Judson: God's Man in Burma

Designed by Jon Kopp and Jamie Leong
Cover and illustrations by Del Thompson

Printed in the United States of America
All rights reserved

ISBN 978-1-57924-625-9

15   14   13   12   11   10   9   8   7   6   5

This book is dedicated to
Catherine Jacobs

Books by Sharon Hambrick

The Arby Jenkins Series
Arby Jenkins
Arby Jenkins, Mighty Mustang
Arby Jenkins, Ready to Roll
Stuart's Run to Faith
Arby Jenkins Meets His Match

The Fig Street Kids Series
Tommy's Clubhouse
Tommy's Rocket
Tommy's Race

The Year of Abi Crim
Adoniram Judson: God's Man in Burma
Brain Games

Contents

1
A Surprise for Father

"Good-bye, Father!" Adoniram Judson waved his small arms above his head and ran down the dirt path.

Father turned in the saddle to wave farewell to his son.

"I know you are just three years old, Adoniram," he said, smiling. "But I am counting on you to be a good boy and to help your mother." He pressed his heels firmly into the horse's sides, and he cantered off down the lane.

"I will, Father," Adoniram said. "I will be very good!"

He stood in the lane until Father was out of sight beyond the elm trees at the end of the path. He started to cry, wiped a hand across his eyes, then felt Mama's hand on his shoulder.

"Come inside, Son," Mama said. She led him up the steps and across the wooden porch. "I have the most wonderful idea."

Adoniram followed Mama inside the parsonage, trying to keep up with her by taking long steps. As they passed Father's study, he stopped and peeked in. He looked up at the sturdy wooden bookshelves and the hundreds of books that sat there. A large black book lay open on Father's desk. Next to the book was a small pile of papers. He knew that the large book was the Bible and that the papers were notes for Father's next sermon.

Adoniram wanted to touch the Bible, but he knew it would be wrong.

"You must never go into my study without permission," Father always said.

Adoniram suddenly remembered Mama's promise of a wonderful idea. She had gone into the kitchen. Maybe she had made a special treat for him!

He ran after Mama to the kitchen. He stood on his tiptoes to look at the tabletop. There was no sign of cookies or a cake. He scrambled up onto a stool and pulled at Mama's apron.

"What is it, Mama?" he asked. He opened his eyes wide and smiled broadly. "What is the wonderful idea? Is it a treat for me?"

Mama poured herself a cup of tea and sipped it thoughtfully. She looked down at Adoniram with a smile.

"No, it's not for you. It's a surprise for Father, but I know you will like it very much too."

Adoniram winced. He remembered the time he had brought Father a handful of dead bugs. "Father doesn't like surprises," he said.

"He will like this one," Mama said. "I promise. He will like it very much."

Mama set her teacup down on the table, untied her apron, and took Adoniram's hand.

"Come with me, Son," she said.

He was surprised when she walked with him straight into Father's study and sat down in

Father's best chair. She took the big Bible from the desk and laid it open on her lap. Then she put her arm out to Adoniram and pulled him close beside her.

"You will learn to read, Adoniram," she said. She ruffled his hair. "I will teach you. You will be able to read a little bit of God's word to Father when he returns from his trip."

Adoniram nestled his head on his mother's shoulder as he stood beside her. He looked down at the open Bible. There were black marks on the white pages, but they meant nothing to him. Could he really learn to read what it said before Father returned?

"Mama," he said. "I am too little to read."

"You are small," she said smiling, "but you are a very smart boy."

Adoniram listened to Mama's lessons. He studied the alphabet and learned the letters *A* and *B* and *C*. He learned to recognize a few words, but some were harder and he had to puzzle out the sounds one by one. After a few days, he was able to understand a little bit of the chapter he was studying.

"Is Father coming home today?" he asked.

"Not today," Mama said.

The next day he could read a few more words. "Is Father coming home today?"

"Soon," Mama said.

The days passed. Then one day, Adoniram ran into the kitchen, the large Bible clutched under his arm.

"Mama!" He put the book down carefully on the kitchen table and looked up at her with shining eyes. "Mama, will you listen, please? I can read the whole chapter!"

Mama rushed over to him. "I knew you could do it," she said. She gave Adoniram a big hug. Just then the front door slammed shut! Adoniram had not even heard it open. He looked up, gasped in surprise, and jumped off Mama's lap.

"Father, you're home!" he said, laughing and jumping. "I have the most wonderful surprise for you!"

Adoniram put his finger on the first word of the chapter and began to read. He read every word of the chapter, making only a few mistakes. When he had finished, he looked up into his father's face. Father's mouth hung open and his eyes were wide.

At first he said nothing. Then he whispered, "You can read!" He picked Adoniram up, swung him around and said it again, much louder, "You can read!"

That night Mama came to tuck Adoniram into bed. He sat up and twined his arms around her neck. "We did it," he said. "We surprised Father."

Later on, he heard Father and Mama talking to each other in the hall outside his bedroom door.

"Our son is going to be a great man," Father said. "A child who can read can become anything. He could become a doctor or a lawyer or even the president of the United States!"

Adoniram did not know what the president was, but he knew he had pleased his father, and that was the very best thing in the world.

2 *Baby Mary*

The next morning Father surprised young Adoniram.

"You may read any book in my study, Son," he said.

Adoniram began to read and read and read. Father's study was filled with books. There were books about plants. There were books about insects. There were books about oceans and animals and famous people. There were also many books about God and about the Bible. Adoniram read so much from these books that he decided to become a pastor like his father.

"Come over here, Johnny," he said to his friend one day. "We are having church."

"It's not Sunday," Johnny said. "I want to play ball."

But Johnny stayed to play church. So did many of the other neighborhood children. Adoniram pretended that he was the pastor. He stood in the yard and pretended to open a Bible. Then he tried to preach like Father did every Sunday. Johnny and the other neighborhood children pretended to listen.

"I want to play ball," Johnny said.

"Not until we finish church," Adoniram said. "Everybody stand and sing, *'Go and Preach My Gospel, saith the Lord.'* "

The little children sang the familiar hymn. As they sang, Adoniram looked over at his house. Mama was smiling down at him from the porch, but she looked tired. She rubbed her hands across her stomach. Adoniram thought that was very funny. He had never seen her do that before.

When the song was finished, he waved at her and ran off to play ball with the other children.

When he got home that evening from playing, Mama was not out on the porch. Father was there.

"There's a surprise for you inside, Son," he said. "Come with me."

Adoniram followed Father to Mama's room and looked in. Mama looked very happy now. He walked up to the bed and looked down. There lay a tiny pink person wrapped in a small blanket.

"Here is your sister, Adoniram. Here is Abigail."

"This is a surprise," Adoniram said. "A very little, pink surprise."

The days passed. Abigail began to crawl and then walk. She and Adoniram began to play together. They became good friends. They liked to run around in the fields, picking flowers and capturing bugs.

"Just don't bring them home to Father," Adoniram told Abigail.

After a while, another baby came into the family. This time it was a boy. His name was Elnathan.

"That is a funny name," Adoniram said.

"Adoniram is a funny name too," Abigail said.

"Yes, but it is also Father's name," Adoniram said.

The next baby that came into the family did not have such a funny name. Her name was Mary.

"Now we have a family with four children," Adoniram told his parents. "When I grow up, I will be a famous doctor and become very rich and take care of all of you."

"I think I will be a doctor," Elnathan said.

"You can't be a doctor," Adoniram said. "You are just a little boy."

"You are a little boy too," Elnathan said.

"Yes, but I am very smart, and Father said I will be a great man!"

"Adoniram." His mother's voice was quiet and firm.

"Yes, ma'am." Adoniram knew what she was going to say.

"You must be more humble," she said. "None of us knows what will happen when we grow older. You never know what God might do. Elnathan might become a doctor, and you might be a very poor man."

That night as he lay in bed, he wondered whether he or Elnathan would be the greater man when they grew up. They would all grow up, of course, he and Elnathan and Abigail and Mary. He tried to imagine what they would look like when they got older, but he just couldn't do it.

Suddenly Adoniram heard a scream. He sat up straight in bed, his whole body trembling.

"Mama!" Adoniram cried. "What is happening?" He jumped out of bed and rushed into the hall. Mama was holding onto Father now. Her long hair hung down around her. Tears ran down her face.

"Mary," she whispered. "My beautiful baby."

Adoniram didn't hear the whole story until the next day. Baby Mary had died in the night.

For weeks, Mama could not eat much. She could not sleep. She sat in her chair and cried. Adoniram picked wild flowers from the field for her.

Abigail tried to help too. She swept the wooden floors of the house, but she was so small she could not sweep everything up. Adoniram and Elnathan worked hard.

Little by little, things returned to normal. One night at dinner, Mama said, "I am thankful for the three beautiful children I have left to me." She looked around the table at Adoniram, Abigail, and Elnathan and smiled. "You must all promise me you will stay close and not move too far away when you grow up."

"I will stay with you always, Mama," Abigail said.

"I will be a doctor, but I will stay close," Elnathan said.

"We will all stay close, Mama," Adoniram said.

3 A Puzzle Book

After a few years, Adoniram began attending the town school. He worked hard on his lessons. He also made many friends. But what he liked most was solving riddles and puzzles.

"Adoniram Judson," his friend Johnny said one day, "you think you can solve any puzzle in the world!" Johnny and a few other boys from the town school gathered around Adoniram. Johnny held up a page from the day's newspaper and waved it under Adoniram's nose.

"I think I can solve any puzzle if I work at it hard enough," Adoniram said.

Johnny stuffed the paper into Adoniram's hands. "Here's one you can't do," he said. "It's so hard the newspaper is offering a prize to the first person who solves it."

"I can do it."

"No, you can't," Johnny said. "The paper is for grownups, not for boys like you. Those people at the newspaper have such a hard puzzle they don't even think grownups can solve it."

Adoniram read the puzzle over. It didn't make any sense to him at all.

"I will have to work on it," he said. He sat right down on the ground and began to think.

"Time for class," the teacher called.

But Adoniram was deep in thought.

"Come on, Adoniram," Johnny said. "You'll be late to class!"

The rest of the day went by slowly. Adoniram said his Greek lesson perfectly. So perfectly in fact that one of the boys clapped for him and said, "Old Virgil did it again."

"My name is Adoniram."

"Yes, I know, but you speak Greek like that Greek scholar we studied."

"It's true," the teacher said. "Adoniram, you really have a knack for the language."

Adoniram blushed with happiness. It wasn't often the teacher gave such praise. "I like to solve puzzles," he said. "Language is sort of like a puzzle. You just have to work it out."

The next day, some of the boys gathered around him.

"How's the puzzle coming, Old Virgil?"

Adoniram smiled. "I mailed my answer on the way to school this morning."

The boys were astonished. "You solved it in one day?"

Adoniram smiled. "It was just a puzzle."

That night at dinner, Father looked stern.

"Adoniram," he said. "Did you send a letter to the newspaper?"

Adoniram wondered how his father would know about that. There hadn't been time for the letter to arrive at the newspaper and for the newspaper to print the name of the winner. He had only mailed his answer this morning!

"Yes, sir," Adoniram said.

"Is this the letter you mailed?" Father pulled the letter from a pocket and laid it on the table. How had Father gotten the letter? Was he angry?

"Mr. Philips at the post office gave it to me. He wasn't sure that the minister's son should be writing letters to the newspaper."

Adoniram's mind raced. Was Father going to reprimand him for thinking he could solve a puzzle meant for grownups, or was he going to praise him for being smart? Adoniram stared intently at Father's face, but could not tell what he was thinking.

Father gazed back at Adoniram, but he said nothing.

"Elnathan," Father said at last, turning to his young son. "Have you finished building your snow sled?"

"Almost," Elnathan said.

Adoniram breathed a great sigh of relief. Father had forgotten about it already! There was only one problem left. His school friends would find out that his answer had never arrived at the newspaper.

"That's all right," Adoniram thought. "I would rather have my friends make fun of me than for Father to be angry."

The next day, Father called Adoniram to his side. "Your answer to that puzzle was quite brilliant," he said. "You are a very smart boy, Adoniram, so I have bought you a book filled with hundreds of puzzles." He held the book out to Adoniram. "I hope you enjoy it."

"Oh, thank you, Father," Adoniram said. "I can't wait to get started on them!"

Father tousled Adoniram's hair. "These are hard puzzles," he said. "But when you finish them, I will get you another book with even harder ones."

Adoniram's eyes shone. "Thank you, Father," he said. "I will solve them all!"

Adoniram ran to his room and opened the book to the first page. "Oh, no," he groaned. He flung himself down on his bed and stared at the ceiling. "It's the arithmetic book for the next grade," he said aloud.

Elnathan came into the room and looked at the book. He laughed. "Well, it's like you said before, Adoniram. You just have to work at it."

Adoniram thought about what Elnathan had said. He was right. If he looked at each arithmetic problem as a little puzzle, he could solve one at a time until the whole book was done."

"I have a puzzle for you," Father said a few days later.

"Please, Father, no more puzzles," Adoniram said. "I have a whole book of arithmetic puzzles I'm working on."

"This one is different," Mr. Judson said. "My friend Mr. Reed heard about your answer to the newspaper puzzle. He knows a very tricky puzzle. Solve it, and he will give you a dollar."

"A whole dollar?" Adoniram said. "I'll do it!"

Father took the folded puzzle from his pocket and passed it to Adoniram. Adoniram read it over.

"This one is hard," he said. "It's impossible."

Mama bustled into the dining room carrying a plate of hot steamy rolls. "Did I hear someone say 'impossible'?" she said. "The Bible says nothing is impossible with God."

"It's a puzzle, Mama," Abigail said. "Adoniram will win a dollar if he solves it."

"Oh," said Mama, smiling. She placed the rolls down on the table. "If I know Adoniram, he'll do just that."

Adoniram shut himself up in his room for a whole day. He could not think of the answer. Some schoolboys shouted up at him to come down and play ball, but he didn't. Abigail knocked on his door and begged him to come and help her feed the chickens.

"I'm thinking about this puzzle," he said.

"Let him think," Mama said.

By the middle of the second day, Mama decided he had thought about the puzzle long enough.

"Come out of your room, Son," she said. "Run around and play with your brother."

Adoniram played with Elnathan. They ran. They jumped. They shouted. Then they started to build a fort out of old corn cobs.

"A good foundation will help make a solid house," Adoniram said, laying cobs out in neat rows. "Then you can pile up the walls and the—"

Adoniram stopped speaking. "I've got it!" he shouted. He jumped up and fell into the cob house. Cobs flew in every direction, but Adoniram didn't stop running until he got to his room so he could write down the answer.

Soon the dollar was safe in his hands. He laid it on the table at dinner time.

"Maybe we can all get a treat with it," he said. "It wasn't *that* hard to do. You just have to work at it."

"And you must remember that nothing is impossible with God," Mama said. "When you have a problem in your life that seems too difficult for you, God will give you wisdom to solve it if you turn to Him."

"It was just a little puzzle, Mama."

"Listen to your mother," Father said. "She is giving you the best advice you will ever get."

"My life doesn't have any problems, Father," Adoniram said. "Everything is just fine."

4 *My Friend Jacob*

For a long time, it seemed as if Adoniram was right. There were no big troubles in his life. He graduated from the town school and decided to go to Providence College.

"Do you have to go to college?" Abigail asked him. "Why can't you stay home and work in the town? I don't want you to go away."

"I want to go to college, Abigail," he said. "Think of all the wonderful things I will learn. Maybe I will be able to study medicine and be a doctor. Or perhaps I will study law and become a lawyer or even president of the United States."

"That would please Father," Abigail said. "Still, I will miss you very much."

"Don't worry, Sis," Adoniram said. "I will only be at college for a few years. Then I will come home and get married and set up a house right over there and you can teach my children to read and write!"

"Your children will probably learn to read by themselves when *they* are three years old," Abigail said.

Adoniram laughed. "Please don't remind me of that. I remember how proud I was that I could read. And now I am going off to college. I will be doing a lot of reading there."

The day arrived for Adoniram to leave. He tossed his trunk of clothes and books onto the top of the coach, then ran back to the house to hug his parents and his brother and sister good-bye.

"I will be home soon," he said. "I love you all."

As the coach moved off, Adoniram looked out the window and waved. Then he settled back into the seat and thought about the wonderful things that were ahead of him at college. "I will work out all the puzzles and problems of college, and everyone will be very proud of me."

Adoniram enjoyed his time at college very much. He studied hard. He learned more Greek and more Latin and more Hebrew. There was more math than he had ever imagined there could be. He studied history and science and grammar. He also made good friends. One of his best friends was Jacob Eames.

"Adoniram, I like you," Jacob said one night. A group of young men were studying in the dormitory. Others were playing games. Some were singing a loud song. "You're a good person, but you have one problem."

"What's that?" Adoniram said. He had come to enjoy problems. He could figure them out easily.

"You believe in God," Jacob said.

Adoniram sat up straight. "What do you mean, Jacob? Of course I believe in God. Don't you?"

"Not me," Jacob said. "It's not fashionable to believe those things any more. Make your own way in the world. You don't need God."

"What are you saying, Jacob?" Adoniram said. "I have never heard anyone speak like this!" He looked around, but no one else seemed alarmed. Some of the young men even nodded their heads in agreement.

Adoniram stopped writing letters to his parents as often. Instead, he began to listen to Jacob Eames. At last, he decided he too would trust in himself instead of in God. He would work out his own life in his own way.

He graduated from college with the highest grades in his class. Then he went home to tell his parents about his new way of life.

His family rushed out to greet him. He had been gone three years!

"Adoniram, you're home!"

Abigail threw her arms around him and cried. Father and Mama both hugged him. Elnathan shook his hand and patted him on the back. "You should see what we've been doing around here while you've been gone," he said.

Adoniram knew he should tell his family right away. "I have something to tell you," he said. "I no longer believe in God."

Mama stared at him for a moment, then turned and quietly walked into the house.

Father stood tall and stern before him.

I will trust in myself to solve this problem, Adoniram thought.

"Have you listened to me preach all those years, Son, and have not come to know the Lord Jesus?" Father said. "Have you thrown off all the training your mother and I have given you? Have you come home to break our hearts?"

Father turned away and walked into the house. Adoniram looked at Abigail and Elnathan.

"That was mean, Adoniram," Abigail said. "Even if you feel that way, you should not have told Mama like that. You have broken her heart."

Abigail and Elnathan walked slowly away from him.

Adoniram decided he would solve this family problem his own way. He would leave. If the family didn't want him around, he would never come back. He would go out into the world and do whatever he wanted.

"I don't need you," he said to the house that stood silently before him. "And I still don't believe in You," he said, looking up into the silent sky.

Adoniram left home. He joined a group of traveling actors. They rode on horses from town to town and put on plays. When they got to a new town, they would find lodging at an inn. Then, when they left that town, they would run off without paying their bill.

They spent all of their time having parties and putting on plays.

"I'm glad my parents don't know what I'm doing," he said to the other actors one night.

"Why?" someone said.

"My mother cries every night because I am an unbeliever! If she knew I was a traveling actor not paying my bills, she would cry all day too!" He took a long drink from his glass and then laughed out loud.

Late that night, he thought of how he had laughed at his mother's sorrow. *Trusting in myself isn't getting me anywhere*, he thought. He remembered the things his friend Jacob Eames had said to him.

"Adoniram," Jacob had said, "You don't need to be a Christian. You're a young man. Have a good time. Be an unbeliever like me!"

Adoniram felt strange. Part of him wanted to run home and hug his mother and tell her he was sorry. But another part of him wanted to keep going down the selfish road he was traveling. He could not sleep, so he packed his things and got on his horse. He rode away from his friends.

I wonder where I am going, he thought as he traveled down the road away from the acting company.

He rode alone for several weeks. He stopped in small villages and met many people. He talked to everyone he met and tried to find the answer to the question: Should I be a Christian or should I trust in myself? One afternoon, he talked for so long it began to get dark.

"I'd better find a place to stay," he said, as he got up from the table and waved good-bye to the people he had met that day.

He trotted his horse a few miles down the road to an inn. There were candles lit inside. It seemed to be a warm and inviting place. He settled his horse into the stable, then went inside to speak to the innkeeper.

"Do you have a room I could rent for the night?" he asked.

"I have just one," said the innkeeper, "but I am afraid it might not be very comfortable."

"Why not?" Adoniram asked.

"Because there is a man in the room next to it who is very, very ill. He groans with pain all day and all night. You might find it quite difficult to sleep."

"Don't worry about that," he said. "I am an actor. I shall pretend I am dead and I won't hear any of it." Adoniram laughed. But the innkeeper did not laugh as he unlocked Adoniram's door with a large brass key.

But Adoniram could not sleep. The man in the next room was in great agony. Adoniram thought of his days as an actor and how he had acted out death scenes. Adoniram tried to picture the man who was lying in the next room in such great pain. It was probably an old man who had lived a long, happy life. Perhaps his family had been traveling together. Maybe they were all in there with him now to help him through this terrible night.

Adoniram began to think about his own death and how horrible it would be if his parents were right and he was wrong.

If the Bible is true, he thought, *then that man next door will be in heaven or hell very soon!* Adoniram was troubled, but he finally drifted off to sleep.

In the morning, when he woke, no sound came from the room next door.

"Perhaps the man is better now and is sleeping," he thought.

When he went to pay his bill, he asked the innkeeper, "How is the man who was so ill? Is he any better?"

The innkeeper shook his head. "I'm sorry to tell you that he died in the night."

Adoniram was stunned. "Oh," he said quietly. "That is very sad. Do you know who it was?"

"Oh, yes," said the innkeeper. "It was a nice young man from Providence College by the name of Jacob Eames."

Adoniram stared at the innkeeper. *Jacob, dead? It couldn't be. If his parents were right and the Bible was true, then Jacob was now in hell!*

Adoniram crumpled down onto the floor. He wept for his dead friend.

"Young man," the innkeeper said, "Did you know Mr. Eames?"

"He was my friend, sir," he said, wiping tears from his face. "And I let him die without Christ." He struggled to his feet, stumbled out of the inn, mounted his horse, and galloped for home.

When he arrived, he was dirty, hungry, and exhausted. He burst in through the front door.

"Mama," he cried, flinging his arms around her, "I am sorry. I have come home to learn about God. I want to know Jesus."

5

Called of God

Adoniram leaned back in his desk chair at Andover Seminary. He ran his hands through his hair and sighed. His friend Samuel walked into the dormitory room and then slammed the door.

"How are you, Judson?" Samuel said, flashing a big smile.

"I don't know, Samuel," Adoniram said. "I am twenty-one years old and thought I knew everything, but the most amazing idea has just occurred to me."

"What is it?" Samuel asked.

Adoniram patted the book that lay open on his desk. "I was just reading a sermon called 'The Star in the East.' This sermon says we should

send people to other countries to be missionaries."

"Sounds crazy," Samuel said. "There's plenty
of church work here in America."

"I know," Adoniram said, "but the idea burns
into my heart."

Samuel grabbed a pile of books from his own
desk, looked over his shoulder at Adoniram,
then quietly left the room.

Adoniram stared at the ceiling. He let his
mind wander to distant lands where people
wore strange clothes and spoke strange languages. After a while, he got up and paced the
dormitory halls.

"Has anyone thought of foreign missions?"
he called out. Young men poked their heads out
of their rooms.

"We're studying, Judson," they said. "Leave
us alone!"

"There are millions of people around the
world who have never heard about Jesus," he
said. "And there is not one American missionary
overseas!"

"We have missions to the American Indians out west," one man answered.

"England is doing the job of foreign missions," another said.

"There is enough church work to do right here," said a third man.

Adoniram could not shake off the thought that God might want him to be a missionary far from America. He left the dormitory and ran out into the woods beyond the seminary.

Cool night air surrounded him while he walked and prayed. Fallen leaves crunched under his feet.

"Oh, God," he said, "show me Thy way."

As he prayed, a Bible verse sprang into his mind: *Go ye into all the world, and preach the gospel to every creature.* Adoniram stopped right where he was and knelt on the forest floor.

"No matter how hard it is," he said, "I will obey God's command to go into the world and preach the gospel."

The next time Adoniram visited home, he was bursting with the news. He knew his family would be happy about his decision to become a foreign missionary. They had all prayed for him so long!

"There are five of us students," he said, his eyes shining. "We are going to obey Christ and become missionaries overseas!"

He was surprised when he looked around the dinner table and saw only sad faces.

"Adoniram," Father said, "I had hoped you would follow me as pastor of our church."

"Please don't do this," Mama said. "If you go away," she paused, "perhaps we will never see you again."

Adoniram looked at Abigail for support. He saw only tears on her face and sadness in her eyes.

Adoniram rose early the next morning and walked down to the town marketplace. He walked among the sellers' stalls, looked at all the familiar faces, saw all the familiar buildings.

He knew that it would be very hard to leave America.

"I am going to become a missionary," he said to the bread seller. "In India, I expect."

The bread man laughed loudly. "Ha, ha," he said. "That's the funniest thing I have ever heard. Hey, Smith, young Judson thinks he can survive in India!"

Soon a crowd of townspeople gathered around him.

"You'll die if you go to India," one man said, slapping him hard on the back. "It is so hot there, you will burn up!"

A large woman bustled her way into the crowd. "This is a foolish idea if I ever heard one," she said. "You won't be able to speak their language. They'll never understand anything you say."

Adoniram eased his way out of the crowd. Some shouted after him that he was crazy, that it would never work, that God didn't intend Americans to live in other places.

He put his hands in his pockets and started for home.

"I know this is God's will for me," he said aloud.

When he arrived at home, his family stared at him anxiously. "There's a letter for you," his father said. "It is from the largest church in Boston!"

Adoniram's hands shook as he opened the letter and quickly read over it.

"They want me to be their assistant pastor," he said. He handed the letter to his mother.

"Why, this is perfect," she said. "You'll be able to serve God and stay close to home at the same time! Let's celebrate by having a special dessert tonight."

Adoniram turned. Tears brimmed in his eyes. He reached out and hugged his mother. "Mama, I will never settle in Boston," he said. "I have much farther than that to go."

"You are certain, Son?" his father asked. "You must go to a foreign land to preach—to be a missionary?"

"I am certain that this is God's plan for me, Father."

Mr. Judson looked at his son for a long time. Then he put his hands on his son's shoulders. One tear dropped onto his wrinkled cheek. "Then we will help you," he said.

Mr. Judson invited a number of pastors to come to a meeting to discuss the idea of foreign missions. Adoniram knew that the men's decisions could affect his whole life. And yet, he found that he could not pay attention to their discussions. Seated directly across from him at the meeting was Ann Hasseltine, the daughter of one of the men. She had brown hair and blue eyes. When she looked up at Adoniram and smiled, Adoniram thought his heart was going to burst with happiness!

"Adoniram," his father said. "Mr. Hasseltine asked you a question."

"I'm sorry, sir," Adoniram said, startled. "I was daydreaming."

Mr. Judson looked from Adoniram to Ann. "Ah," he said. "I understand."

Adoniram and Ann became friends. They wrote letters to each other. Soon Adoniram found himself sitting at his writing table late one night.

"Dear Mr. Hasseltine," he wrote, "I must ask you whether you can part with your daughter next spring. Will you allow her to go to a far-away country to be a missionary's wife? There will be danger, poverty, insults, and maybe even death, but it is for the sake of the Lord Jesus Christ and for the millions of lost souls over-seas."

When he received Mr. Hasseltine's reply, he jumped up and shouted. "I'm getting married," he said. He ran through the house and banged on all the doors. "I'm going to marry Ann!"

"It is a hard work you are undertaking, son," his father said. "You will need a good wife like Ann."

"Ann is a wonderful girl," his mother said. "Take good care of her."

Adoniram hugged both his parents tightly. "Don't worry. I won't let anything bad happen to her."

6

In the Dungeon

Adoniram struggled to wake up. He hurt all over and wondered why it was so dark and why the ground was moving under him. His throat was dry and his stomach ached with hunger.

"Water, please, Mama," he said.

Then he remembered. His mother was thousands of miles away. Ann was thousands of miles away. All his friends were in America, and he was somewhere on the ocean in a ship that had been captured by pirates!

Adoniram closed his eyes. He could picture Ann's face as she had shyly said good-bye to him a few weeks before. The other four young men who wanted to be missionaries had also gathered with him as he had boarded this boat.

"Go to England," they had said. "Tell them we want to go to India like their great missionary William Carey. Tell them we need their help."

Adoniram groaned in pain. "I don't even know where I am or where I am going."

For days he just sat there, smelling the foul air, longing for something to eat. His eyes became accustomed to the dim light, and he could see the other prisoners. They all looked the same—tired, sad, and frightened.

"I wonder what they are going to do with us," Adoniram said aloud. But no one answered. No one could understand him, and he could not understand the loud and long conversations that were held in Spanish.

"What good was it that I studied Latin, Greek, and Hebrew at school?" he said. "Those languages won't do me any good at all."

Everyone was seasick. The place smelled worse and worse every day.

"As long as I live," Adoniram said, "this is the worst thing that will ever happen to me. I should cheer up and know that this is as bad as it gets."

Adoniram asked God to help him. He pulled his Hebrew Bible out of his baggage and began to read it aloud in Latin, translating from Hebrew in his mind as he went along.

He read aloud in Latin for several hours.

"Young man," the ship's doctor said to him in Latin. "Why didn't you tell me you could speak the old tongue?"

Adoniram smiled. "I never thought about it," he said. "I assumed everyone here knew only Spanish."

He explained to the doctor that he was not a part of the crew.

"I am an American missionary on my way to London," he said.

"Well, I suppose a missionary will not cause trouble to the pirates. You may come on deck. I'm sure you will feel much better up there."

"Thank you, doctor," Adoniram replied. "I think you have saved my life." Adoniram looked down at his Hebrew Bible. "I guess knowing those ancient languages is important!"

The doctor helped him crawl up the ladder. What a tremendous relief it was to stand on the deck and feel the cold salty sea air pouring over his face. Adoniram threw himself down on the deck and slept.

When he woke up, he thanked God for sparing his life in the filthy hold.

"Now I know You can take care of me wherever I go in all the world."

Many days passed. At last Adoniram saw land.

Spain looked different from anything Adoniram had ever seen in America. The trees were different. The houses were different. The people wore different kinds of clothes. Adoniram felt very strange. He had not been able to change his clothes in a long time. He had not been able to keep clean. He wanted to stop and clean up, but he and the ship's crew were immediately sent to Bayonne, a town in France.

"This is terrible," Adoniram thought. "The mission board is waiting for me to arrive in London. My family and my friends don't know where I am. Ann is probably very worried!"

In France the captives were paraded through the street. Adoniram did not know where he was being taken, but he knew that he did not want to go there. He began shouting in English. Maybe someone in the crowd would understand him.

"Help me!" he shouted. "I am an American. I am not a crew member. I want to go home."

No one seemed to understand. He shouted more. He shouted anything he could think of.

"I am a missionary. I am engaged to Ann Hasseltine. I have a brother with the funny name of Elnathan. Once I was a traveling actor. When I was a little boy, I gave my father a handful of dead bugs and knocked over a cob house! I learned to read when I was three years old!"

Still no one listened. He began to shout about how evil it was to be a pirate and how wrong it was to take people captive and put them below the deck of a ship!

Suddenly a man in a black cloak sidled up to him. "Lower your voice," the man said in English. Adoniram gasped in surprise. English!

"I am from Philadelphia," said the man. "Go with the guards now, and I will do what I can to rescue you."

Adoniram nodded, thanked the man, and then continued on his way with the ship's crew, saying nothing for the rest of the way.

They arrived at a large gray prison. He was led down, down, down to a dark, dismal dungeon. There were no beds. A dim lamp gave out a pitiful light. Straw was spread around the walls. Adoniram tried to make himself a little pile of straw to sit on.

"I wonder what bugs have been crawling in this straw," Adoniram said. He shivered in the dampness of the place and felt sick breathing the sour-smelling air. He paced up and down the cell for hours, wondering what was going on outside and whether the man from Philadelphia had been telling the truth. What if the man had really been a friend of the pirates? If that were true, then Adoniram would be stuck in this dungeon forever. He would grow old and die here and never see Ann or his family or friends again.

I will never get to be a missionary, he thought. *All my trouble will have been for nothing, and then I will die.*

He grew tired of pacing, but he did not stop. He did not want to lie down in the old straw.

If I ever get out of here, I am going straight to London and then straight home to marry Ann. Then we will go east to be missionaries and forget all about prisons forever. But then, what if I am here for so long that Ann gives up on me and marries someone else? This terrible thought raced through his mind and gave him a headache.

He leaned against one of the pillars in the middle of the room. Just then a loud screeching noise shattered the silence. It was the noise of the old rusty door being opened. Two men entered. One was the jailer, but who was the other man? Adoniram looked closely at the man.

It was the man from Philadelphia.

Adoniram leaned against the pillar silently. He did not know what to do. Should I call out and tell him I'm here? Or should I wait quietly and see what he is going to do?

Adoniram did nothing. He just stared at the man and silently prayed to God for rescue.

The American man spoke quietly to the jailer. Then he spoke loudly in English, "Let me take a look around and see if I know any of these poor men." The American man walked slowly around the room, holding up his lamp in front of each man's face. He looked into Adoniram's face. Adoniram gave him a tight smile and nodded. The man turned away from him.

"No," the man said loudly. "There's no one here that I recognize."

Adoniram was about to shout out, but just as he opened his mouth, the American man turned quickly, opened his enormous black cloak and flung it around him.

He is smuggling me out, thought Adoniram. The American man began to walk slowly. Adoniram made himself as small as he could and walked very close to the man. What if someone noticed what was happening?

Suddenly, Adoniram realized he was out of the prison and in the street. The American gentleman opened his black cloak to let him out. "Run," the man said.

Adoniram ran down to the wharf. He got on an American ship and collapsed on a cot, breathing hard. Before he fell asleep, he thanked God for taking care of him even in prison.

"I never want to be in prison again," he said. "But at least I know God will protect me in bad times. Now all I need to do is get to London to speak with that mission board."

London was a great city. Adoniram was very glad that people there spoke English.

"There are five of us," he told the London Missionary Society. "We have promised God we will spend our lives preaching about Jesus Christ in foreign lands. Several pastors in America have asked me to come here and seek your help. Will you send us to India?"

The men talked and prayed. Adoniram paced the halls. He looked into the room, but the men were still talking. He walked around London. Finally, there was news.

"There is trouble between England and America," the men said. "We might even be at war soon. We think it is best if the American churches send out their own missionaries."

Adoniram turned to go. He boarded the ship with a heavy heart. He had come all this way, been captured by pirates, stashed in a dungeon—all for nothing! All the way home, he prayed, "Father, help us."

Ann met the ship. Her face was bright and happy.

"I am so happy to see you," he said, "but I feel as if I have accomplished nothing. There is no one to help us go. Our future is very dim."

Ann shook her head. "No, Adoniram," she said. "Our future is as bright as all the promises of God. You must trust Him—not the mission boards—to get you to India."

Adoniram smiled down at the small woman by his side.

"You're right," Adoniram said. "I think I shall marry you right away so you can keep giving me such good advice."

7 *The Caravan*

"Good-bye, Ann! Good-bye, Adoniram!" friends shouted from the dock as the newly married Mr. and Mrs. Judson boarded the *Caravan*. They had been married for only two weeks, and they were going to India!

Ann stood at the rail and waved back happily. Her friend Harriet Newell stood beside her. Harriet had been married to Samuel Newell a short time also.

"We have pretty wives," Adoniram said to Samuel.

"Yes, we do," Samuel said. "We shall all grow old together in India."

The four of them laughed together, then went to join the captain at his table for dinner.

When they looked out the next morning, they could see nothing but miles of water in every direction. Waves sloshed against the sides of the boat and splashed salt spray in their faces and hair.

"Here we go!" Adoniram cried. "What a great adventure!"

For four months, the *Caravan* sailed across the ocean. There were storms and choppy seas. They got sick. They got better. They got sick again.

"We'll trust God through everything," Adoniram told Ann. "God protected me in the French prison, and He will take care of us on this journey."

"We'll have a nice little home in India soon," Ann said. "Everything will be perfect."

"I have heard good things about India," Harriet said. "It is ruled by the English. Samuel and I heard about a country close to India that is ruled by a cruel king."

"Burma," said Samuel. "The king there kills people for no reason at all!"

Ann shivered. "Let's be glad we aren't going there," she said.

The *Caravan* rounded the coast of Africa, leaving the Atlantic Ocean.

"The Indian Ocean is named for India," Adoniram said. "We must be almost home."

"Home," said Ann. She grabbed her friend Harriet's hand and smiled. "It will be nice to be on the ground again, won't it, Harriet?"

"Oh, yes," Harriet said. "I do not feel so well. I will feel much better when I can walk on something solid that doesn't move!"

At last the day came.

"There's India," the captain said to the four missionaries. "And I think I see someone who has come to meet you."

The great English missionary William Carey was on the dock to meet them.

"Everything will be fine now," Adoniram said.

But everything was not fine. Soon after they had settled into the mission house, a government official arrived. He wore a fancy coat and carried a sword.

"You must leave India at once," the man said. "We want no more missionaries here."

Adoniram jumped to his feet. "What do you mean?" he said. "England rules India. Surely England wants India reached for Jesus Christ."

The government man cleared his throat loudly. "My dear young man," he said. "India is ruled by the East India Company. The Company does not want the natives to become Christians. If they do, there might be trouble between those who become Christians and those who do not." He straightened up and put his hand on his sword hilt. "We don't want any trouble, now, do we?"

Adoniram looked around the room. The other missionaries stared back at him with wide open eyes. "Think of the trouble that will come to the people of India if they do not hear the gospel," he said.

The man in the fancy coat shook his head. "You cannot stay here," he said. "Go back to America where you belong."

"Please excuse us, sir," Adoniram said. "My friends and I need to pray."

Adoniram and Ann, Samuel and Harriet knelt together on the floor. They clasped their hands together and prayed fervently.

"Dear Father," Samuel prayed. "We have come so far to preach Jesus Christ. Please help us find a place we can serve you."

Adoniram spoke first. "May we settle on the island of Mauritius?"

"Yes," said the government man. "That is a good idea. A ship is going there soon, but there is room for only two more passengers. The other two of you must stay behind until another ship comes."

Samuel pulled Adoniram aside and spoke to him quietly. Adoniram nodded.

"We will go to Mauritius," Samuel said to the government man. "My wife Harriet is ill. She needs to be done with traveling as soon as possible."

Ann hugged Harriet good-bye. "We will be with you soon," she said to her friend. "Then we will work together, build a mission, raise families, and serve the Lord all our lives."

They waved until the boat was out of sight. Ann sighed. Then she and Adoniram walked back to the mission house.

Time passed quickly. Soon Adoniram and Ann boarded another ship bound for Mauritius.

"I can't wait to see Harriet again," Ann said as they approached the island coast. They hurried to retrieve their baggage and climbed down the ladder to the dock.

Samuel stood on the dock alone. His eyes were red. His face was weary and sad.

"Where is Harriet?" Ann said. She looked up and down the dock. "Where is my friend, Samuel?"

Samuel began to cry. "Harriet is dead," he said. Adoniram and Ann gathered him into a hug and cried with him. "She loved Jesus and wanted to tell all these people about Him, but now—now she is gone."

That afternoon they visited the cemetery. Adoniram prayed with Samuel. Ann gathered wild flowers and placed them on Harriet's grave. "Good-bye, my dear friend," she said.

"I cannot stay here," Samuel said.

Adoniram nodded. "Go in peace, my friend. God will give you rest and help."

After four months Adoniram and Ann were also ready to leave.

"I am restless here," Adoniram said. "We spend all our time working with the English soldiers. There are thousands of men who can preach the gospel in English and very few who can preach to the native people. We must go further east."

"All I want is a little spot that I can call my own," Ann said. She smiled at her husband, took a last long look at the beautiful island of Mauritius, then walked into the house to pack their things. In a few days they were back at the port in India.

"You may not stay here," the government official told them as they descended from the ship onto Indian soil.

"We know we cannot stay in India," Adoniram said. "We are just waiting for a ship to take us further east."

"No," the man said. "That won't be possible. There is a ship at anchor in the harbor. It is leaving for England tonight. You two will be on that ship. You will go to England and from there you will go on to America."

The man stomped away from them, his silver sword shining in the sunlight. Adoniram looked at Ann.

"I know God does not want us to go back to America yet, Ann," Adoniram said. "We must run away from India!"

"Where will we go?" Ann asked.

"Anywhere we can," Adoniram said. "God will show us."

Adoniram and Ann rushed down to the harbor. They asked at ship after ship, but every ship was heading to a port controlled by the

East India Company. If they boarded any of those ships, they would be found and sent back to England or America.

Hours passed. Ann slumped down onto a wooden bench beneath a large shade tree. She shaded her eyes with her hand and looked out across the harbor. Suddenly, a little ship caught her attention.

"Look, Adoniram," Ann said. "There's a small boat just behind that big ship there. Let's ask the captain where he is going."

They approached the captain of the *Georgianna*.

"Where are you bound?" Adoniram asked.

"Nowhere you two nice folks want to go," the captain said. "I'm heading out to hostile territory, if you know what I mean." He coughed loudly and spat tobacco juice over the side of the ship.

"Where?" asked Adoniram.

"Burma," said the captain.

Ann gasped. Adoniram bit his lip and nodded his head. He turned and looked around the harbor. Every other vessel would take them away from where they believed God wanted them to work. This was the only ship in the whole harbor that was heading toward a land where they could reach heathen people for Christ.

"Adoniram," Ann said, pulling on his sleeve. "Remember what we heard about the king of Burma. He is cruel. He kills people he doesn't like!"

"That is true," Adoniram nodded. "But I believe God will take care of us if we do what He wants us to do." He looked deeply into Ann's eyes. "We can go to Burma or we can go home to America. What does God want us to do?"

Ann and Adoniram bowed their heads in prayer. They asked God to show them what to do. When they finished praying, Ann's face was bright and happy. Adoniram's was too.

"Captain," he said, "do you have room for two passengers?"

"I do," he said. "But the ride will be stormy, and I have no accommodations for you. You must live in a canvas tent on the deck."

Adoniram looked at Ann. For a woman accustomed to a comfortable home in New England, perhaps it would be too much for her to live in a tent. But Ann smiled and nodded. "With God nothing is impossible," she said.

"Good," said Adoniram. "Then we shall go to Burma. We shall tell the people there of the Savior. Maybe we will even tell the cruel king."

The captain looked over the two young people. "You're crazy," he said. "But I like you. Get on board. We sail in an hour."

8
Rangoon

"Dear God, help us!" Ann cried into the stormy night. Thunder crashed and lightning split the sky around them, great bolts spearing the sea. The tossing waves plunged the *Georgianna* up to their crests and then down into massive water valleys.

Adoniram rushed to Ann's side. She was feverish, but could not keep warm. She was exhausted, but could not sleep. Her eyes were wide with fear. "Help me, Adoniram," she said. "I think I am going to die."

Adoniram thought so too. The boat tossed violently. There was no doctor on board the little ship. There was no medicine. Adoniram felt helpless.

"I shall be with Harriet in heaven soon," Ann said in a whisper. "What will you do?"

Adoniram looked from his wife's face up into the black night sky. No stars could be seen, and the moon was hidden. "Do not be hid from me, O God," he said. "Preserve Ann's life, I pray." Then he considered what Ann had said. What would he do if she were taken from him in death?

"Whether you live or die, I will reach the Burmese people for Jesus Christ," he said. He laid his hand on her hot forehead and smoothed her hair away from her face. "But Ann, I want you to live and serve the Lord with me."

"I shall try to live," Ann said. She sighed deeply. Then she began to cough and could not stop. Thunder crashed. Adoniram held his wife in his arms on the deck of the storm-tossed ship.

Days passed in this way. Adoniram paced up and down the deck of the ship, a difficult task since the boat was so unsteady. He quoted Bible verses over and over to himself:

For with God nothing shall be impossible.

I can do all things through Christ which strengtheneth me.

I will never leave thee, nor forsake thee.

Adoniram glanced over the little ship, tossing so fragilely on the waves. He looked down at his wife and watched her struggling to breathe. He looked up into the rigging. A man was at the top of the mast. He was waving his arms and shouting, "Land, land!"

Adoniram put his hand to his brow and looked out across the sea. "It's Burma," he whispered. He leaned over Ann and whispered into her ear. "We've made it. We're in Burma."

Ann moved a little. "I am so sick, Adoniram," she said.

The ship drew closer to the shore, and the city of Rangoon came into sight.

"It looks like any other city," Adoniram said. But as the distance between the boat and the shore closed, it began to look different.

"What is that huge golden spire?" Adoniram asked the captain.

"That, my friend, is the great pagoda. That's where the people worship. That pagoda's been here for centuries. It'll be a hard job for you two young people to take anyone away from worshiping there." He laughed. "I don't suppose your bags are full of gold to build a golden church!"

Adoniram did not laugh.

"We have something better than gold, Captain," Adoniram said. "We bring news of a Savior."

Ann could not walk, so she was placed in an arm chair and carried through the streets by four men. Women crowded around the chair in a tight crush. They poked at her long English-style dress and lifted it up to see her shoes.

"Please," Adoniram said to the people. "Give my wife some room to breathe. She is not well."

But the people continued to push and shove. They touched her long dress and the laces on her bonnet. Someone peeked under her bonnet and shrieked with laughter!

The Burmese people were a lovely deep brown color. Adoniram knew they were laughing at Ann's pale white skin. He knew that the jostling and poking must be making her even more ill than she already was.

Adoniram rushed to the front of the crowd and made signs to the men who were carrying Ann that they must move faster. Still, it seemed like hours passed before they arrived at the English mission house.

"Surely the English missionaries will help us here like Mr. Carey helped us in India," Ann whispered. Her hand hung down, and when Adoniram helped her out of the chair, she collapsed into his arms.

"Hello!" Adoniram shouted into the house. "We're here!" There was no answer. He lowered Ann gently to the ground. "Stay here," he said to Ann. "I'll find them."

Adoniram looked everywhere. "They've gone," he said at last. "I guess we have the whole place to ourselves."

Adoniram carried Ann into the house and laid her on a bed. "Get some sleep, my dear," he said. Then he ran back outside to get their baggage. He piled it against the wall.

"Well, sweetheart, we're home," he said to Ann. He smoothed her hair away from her eyes and sponged her face with a damp cloth. "We're in Burma at last. We have found God's place for us."

"It took such a long time," Ann said softly. Her eyes were closed, and she lay quite still.

"Yes," Adoniram said. "It was eighteen long months ago that we left America. But now we are home."

He looked around the empty mission house. "It is strange," he said. "This is just a simple building. But in a few years, it will be full of little children of our own. Burmese people who have come to Christ will visit us, and every day we will all speak and sing and pray together in that strange language we heard outside. A great church will be built for Jesus Christ here. Isn't that wonderful, Ann?"

There was no answer. Adoniram looked down at her and smiled. She was sleeping.

9
The Zayat

Adoniram left the mission house early the next morning while Ann was still asleep. He walked briskly up and down the streets of Rangoon. He stared up at the huge golden spire that rose into the bright blue sky. Lines of Buddhist priests in bare feet and orange robes chanted as they walked past him toward the pagoda. Old women and little children laid bowls of rice and bunches of flowers at the feet of stone idols.

Everywhere were brown-skinned people with straight black hair and long colorful robes. All of them spoke the strange language he had heard the night before.

"Ann, this is the most extraordinary place," Adoniram said as he burst into the house that evening. "Why are you standing? What are you doing? You should be in bed."

"I am making you some supper," Ann said, smiling. "A woman brought me some rice and fish. See?" She turned from her work in the small mission house kitchen. "I am feeling much better now that I am on solid ground. Did you learn anything today?"

Adoniram grabbed a chair and sat down at the kitchen table. "Oh, Ann," he said. "I learned so much by watching the people, but I must learn the language so I can talk with them!"

Adoniram found an old man who would help him. The man did not speak any English, and Adoniram spoke no Burmese. The two men communicated with each other by pointing to pictures and saying the word.

He learned the words for everyday Burmese things—tiger, waterfall, jungle, forest, spider, rat, pagoda, priest, offering. He learned that the golden pagoda was called Shway Dagon. He learned that the great river that poured through

Rangoon and out into the Indian Ocean was called the Irrawaddy.

After a while he was able to understand the old teacher. "Our people are Buddhists," the man told Adoniram. "We worship many gods."

"Do the gods promise you eternal life in heaven?" Adoniram asked.

The teacher laughed. "Oh, no, teacher. We do not believe in a place called heaven. But if I am a good man, perhaps I shall be reborn as a rich man in my next life."

Adoniram did not laugh. He knew that each man has only one life and that only the true God can forgive sins and grant eternal life.

"Burmese is the hardest thing I've ever had to learn," Adoniram told Ann that night. "And it's even harder to write. The letters are so curvy and different from English."

Ann kissed Adoniram on the cheek. "You can do it." she said. "Burmese is just another puzzle for you to solve."

Adoniram grimaced. "I have solved many puzzles in my life, but this language is the hardest puzzle I've ever seen." He looked up at Ann. "God will help us learn this language. I know He wants me to translate the Bible into Burmese, Ann. Then the people will be able to read God's own word for themselves."

Ann picked up the large black Bible that lay open on the kitchen table and flipped through the pages to the very last one. "Adoniram," she said, "there are over one thousand pages in this book! Do you really think you can learn Burmese well enough to translate all of this? It will take years!"

"I think it will take my whole life," Adoniram said. He sat down on a chair and stretched his legs out before him. He clasped his hands behind his head and stared up at the ceiling. A black bat hung upside down in the corner of the house, and a line of spiders marched along the wall. "But I believe that someday there will be a church of one hundred Christian Burmese who have the Bible in their own language."

Soon Adoniram knew enough Burmese to tell his teacher the gospel. The teacher's eyes grew wide as he heard about the Savior.

"Are you saying that all who are not followers of Jesus Christ are lost in their sins?" the man asked.

"Yes," said Adoniram. "That is what I mean."

The man slumped down in this chair. "This is a very hard saying," he said. "If it is so, then everyone around me who dies is lost. There are no Burmese who love Jesus Christ."

"Yes," Adoniram said. "It is a very hard thing indeed. That is why I have left my family and my friends and my country and traveled around the world to tell you about Him."

The old man looked down at his hands in his lap. He wiped a tear from his eye and coughed. "You are right," he said. "You have given up everything to come to us. You must love Jesus Christ very much."

"Yes," said Adoniram. "And I want you to love Him too."

"I shall think about this," the man said, "and you should build a zayat if you want people to hear about this Jesus."

"What is a zayat, Teacher?" Adoniram asked.

"It is a house for preaching and discussing religion. We Burmese people are used to gathering in zayats. You should build one to tell us about Jesus."

Over the next several weeks, Adoniram divided his time between learning Burmese and building a zayat. He gathered bamboo for the building and long sheaves of dried grass for the thatched roof. He hired Burmese workers to help him build.

Adoniram told the workers about Christ. He talked and he worked. His hands grew sore, and his voice became hoarse.

"Look at those red, blistered hands," Ann said one evening. "I thought you were a preacher, not a builder."

"Right now I am a zayat builder," Adoniram said, laughing. He plunged his hands into a bucket of water Ann brought to him. "Ah, that's much better," he said.

"You need those hands if you are going to translate the Bible," she said. "But tell me, how is the zayat work coming?"

"It is almost finished," he said. "I had several helpers today, but I have to say I have never built a house up on stilts before. At least the stilts are only four feet high. Otherwise I might fall out and break my head!"

"Don't do that," Ann said. "There is too much to lose inside that head. If you cracked your head, you might forget all the Burmese you know, and we'd have to start all over again."

Adoniram and his helpers finished building the zayat. Soon people came to talk to him. They talked about their own religion. They talked about God. They even listened as Adoniram spoke about the Lord Jesus Christ.

But no one believed.

Days and then months passed. Ann worked in the house. Adoniram sat in the zayat and preached to everyone who came in. In the rainy season, the thatched roof would sometimes leak. Adoniram would hire workers to help him fix the leaks. "There is only one God," he told the workers. "And He Himself has paid the penalty for your sins."

Every day Adoniram sat on a grass mat in the front room of the zayat. A hot wind blew through the open door.

"Come in," Adoniram called to the passing people. "Come in and hear how you can be saved."

Some people looked up from the dusty dirt road and smiled.

"You are crazy, Jesus Christ's man," shouted one.

Hour after hour, Adoniram sat, alert for any interest. It would have been so easy to go back to the house and read a book or help Ann with the household chores, but he did not.

"If I leave for one moment, perhaps I will lose the chance to tell someone about Jesus."

Six years passed in this way. Adoniram sat in the zayat all day. Sometimes people came in to

talk or argue about religion. Sometimes one came. Sometimes many came.

"But they don't listen, Ann," Adoniram said one night. "They seem to be entertained by a white man speaking their language."

"Don't worry," Ann said. "God has a people in this city."

"But we have been here for six years and not one person has trusted in Jesus."

Ann rubbed his shoulders and whispered into his ear, "Nothing is impossible with God."

In the morning Adoniram returned to the zayat. He walked over the dew-wet grass, through the hot air, through the dusty streets. He climbed up the ladder to the zayat door and went in.

"Are you the teacher?" a man asked.

Adoniram was startled to hear a voice in the zayat.

"Yes," he said. He moved over to where the voice was coming from and saw a man standing in a far corner. "I am the teacher. Do you wish to hear about the Lord Jesus Christ?"

"I do," said the man. "I have very many sins, and I am afraid to die."

Adoniram beckoned to the man to sit down next to him on the grass mats. "Why are you afraid of death?" he asked.

"Because I know there is a great punishment in store for me," the man said. "But I have heard that you know a way to escape the punishment."

Adoniram smiled. "I do," he said. "What is your name?"

"My name is Moung Nau," the man said. "May I sit down and hear about Jesus?"

"Yes," Adoniram said. "Please sit down."

The next Sunday, Adoniram, Ann, Moung Nau, and a few of his friends gathered at the edge of a small pond. A huge idol of Buddha stood on the far bank of the pond.

"Moung Nau," Adoniram said. "Do you believe in the Lord Jesus Christ?"

"I believe all Jesus Christ has said, and I am ready to obey everything He has commanded."

"What if your family and friends are unhappy with your new religion? Will you turn away?" Adoniram looked deeply into Moung Nau's eyes.

"I wish there were more Burmese believers," Moung Nau said, "but I will stick to Jesus Christ even if no one else ever comes to Him."

Adoniram and Moung Nau waded out into the cool water of the pond. Adoniram prayed a prayer of Thanksgiving to God for saving a Burmese soul. Then he baptized Moung Nau.

"I am so happy," he told Ann and Moung Nau. "Now there is a little church of three of us who follow Christ."

"It is a little church," Ann said. "But the God who builds it is great."

Days later a man named Moung Thah-lah climbed the ladder and bounded into the zayat.

"Teacher," he said, "I have heard that there is forgiveness of sin and eternal life in heaven. This is something I wish to have." Moung Thah-lah stood before Adoniram and breathed heavily as if he had been running a long way to hear good news.

"You must believe on the Son of God," Adoniram told him. "His name is Jesus. Sit down and I will tell you all about Him."

Moung Thah-lah listened. "I wish to believe in Jesus Christ," he said, "but I am afraid I will be rejected by my family if I tell them I have turned to Christ."

Adoniram stood up and walked over to his desk. He opened his Bible and began to work again on the translation of the Scriptures. "I am sorry you are not ready to become a Christian," he said.

"But I am ready!" Moung Thah-lah said.

"You are not." Adoniram continued to write. "You will be ready when you love Jesus more than you fear people."

Moung Thah-lah went away sadly that day, but the next day he was back. "I am ready to follow Jesus no matter what," he said smiling.

A few days later a poor fisherman entered the zayat. "I am Moung Ing," he said. "I have heard about this new religion, and I wish to learn more."

"You are welcome here," Adoniram said. He began to share the gospel with Moung Ing. By now Adoniram could speak Burmese quite well. He could explain the truths of Christ's death and resurrection, forgiveness of sin, and eternal life.

After listening to Adoniram, Moung Ing stood. He looked around the bamboo room. Then he walked over to the window and looked out. He could see the pagoda's spire from where he stood.

"I am amazed by what you are telling me, Teacher," he said. "All my life I have believed in Buddhism, but you tell me it is false and will lead me to hell. I want to know more about Jesus Christ."

A few days later Moung Ing came back to the zayat. "I have studied the book of Matthew you gave me in my language. I thank you for translating it for me. It has given me the understanding I need to follow Jesus. When I think about Christ, I know I love Him more than I love my own life! I wish to be baptized."

"Our little church is growing," Ann said, smiling as she and Adoniram walked home from another baptismal service at the edge of the pond.

"That's because our great God is building it," Adoniram said.

One day a large man climbed the ladder, stepped into the zayat and stood before Adoniram. He bowed slightly to him. Adoniram bowed in return.

"I am a professor," the man said. "My name is Moung Shwa-gnong."

"I am Adoniram Judson," Adoniram said. "I teach the Christian religion. May I tell you about Jesus Christ?"

Moung Shwa-gnong refused to sit. Instead, he remained standing and stared straight into Adoniram's eyes.

"Eight years ago, I heard about the idea of an eternal god," Moung Shwa-gnong said. "It has bothered me ever since then, because if it is true that there is one eternal god, then everything I have learned in Buddhism is false."

Adoniram talked with him all day, but he would not turn to Christ. "This is a good religion," he said. "This makes sense. I agree that it is right."

"Will you follow Jesus?" Adoniram asked.

"No," Moung Shwa-gnong said, "If it is known that I am learning about Christianity, I will be in great trouble. I am an important man in this city. The governor will be angry."

For many days Moung Shwa-gnong did not come back to the zayat. Then one day, he climbed up the steps again and faced Adoniram.

"I came to tell you that I cannot come back here again," the professor said. "I am afraid of the governor."

"You have learned so much about the Savior, my friend," Adoniram said. "Can you really turn your back on Him now?"

"The governor may kill me if I turn to Jesus," Moung Shwa-gnong said. "I do not wish to die." He turned and backed down the ladder. "I will not come back to see you any more," he said.

10
The Golden Feet

"I want to go to Ava," Adoniram said. He paced back and forth across the kitchen.

"Why?" Ann shivered. "That's where the king lives."

"He is the man I am going to see."

Ann dropped the glass she was holding. It shattered on the floor. She bustled around to pick up the sharp glass pieces.

"Sit down, Ann," Adoniram said. "I'll clean the floor. I shouldn't have surprised you like that!"

Adoniram began picking up the shards of glass. "Things are getting hard for our little group of believers here in Rangoon," he said. "But if we are able to meet with the king and obtain his favor, then we will be able to preach anywhere in Burma we want, and the Buddhist priests will be forced to leave the new Christians alone."

"It is so hard for our believers," Ann said. "They are ridiculed and threatened every day. But the king is so powerful! He could have you killed if he doesn't like you. Do you think it's safe to go there, Adoniram?"

Adoniram finished picking up the broken glass. Then he sat back down by Ann at the table. He took her hands in his own and looked into her eyes.

"Every day I tell my little group of believers that they must not fear man. That they must love Christ no matter what happens to them. How can I tell them that if I am afraid to see the king?"

"You are right," Ann said. "We cannot tell the Burmese Christians to trust God if we are not willing to do the same. You must go to the king, but must you go alone?"

"No, the new missionary Dr. Price has agreed to go with me. He is also dedicated to the Lord Jesus. He is a faithful man, and I know he will be a great help to me on the way. Pray for us, Ann. Pray for us every day."

Adoniram and Dr. Price bought a boat. It was six feet wide and forty feet long. They loaded their things on the bamboo deck and got aboard.

Adoniram turned to Ann. "The last time I waved good-bye to you, I was going off to London and was captured by pirates," Adoniram said.

"Let us hope this trip will be an easier one," Ann said.

They shoved the boat off into the great Irrawaddy River and began the three hundred fifty mile trip up the river to Ava, Burma's capital city.

"What a beautiful country this is, John," Adoniram said.

"It is beautiful," Dr. Price agreed. "And think how much better it will be if God grants us His favor before the king."

Ava was a large city, bustling with commerce, with education, with religion. Adoniram and Dr. Price met many people. Most were Burmese, but some were foreigners like themselves. They met many government officials, but it was not as simple to meet the king.

"He is busy," a government man said.

"He is busy again," he said the next day.

Days passed. Adoniram and Dr. Price began to wonder if they would ever be able to see the king. They saw the army. They saw important generals. Elephants carried dignitaries into the city.

Adoniram and Dr. Price told everyone they met about the Lord Jesus Christ. They gave away copies of tracts they had written and parts of the New Testament that Adoniram had translated into Burmese. But they did not see the king.

"Should we go home?" Dr. Price said. "Perhaps we made a mistake in coming."

"Let's wait a little longer," Adoniram said.

At last a man was sent to them from the palace. "You may see the Golden Monarch tomorrow, but you must not approach his majesty unless you are prepared to offer him a handsome present."

"We have a wonderful gift for the king," Dr. Price said. "It is an English copy of our Holy Book, the Bible. It is covered in solid gold."

"That will be a nice gift," the government official agreed. "But I cannot promise that the Golden Face will smile on this book."

That night, Dr. Price and Adoniram drank tea in their room. Adoniram's hands were trembling with excitement. "John," he said, "we have come to the heart of one of the world's great kingdoms, and tomorrow we are going to make an offer of the gospel to the king himself."

"Yes," said Dr. Price. "And if the king approves the gospel, it will fly everywhere with great speed and power."

The next morning, Dr. Price and Adoniram rushed to the palace.

"Today we will get freedom to preach the gospel all over Burma!" Dr. Price said.

They followed a richly dressed court official through courtyards, through gardens, through halls, until they reached the massive throne room in the Golden Palace.

The huge room was crowded with important government officials, but the throne itself was empty. Dr. Price and Adoniram knelt on the floor near the elevated throne. Adoniram looked over the huge hall. Massive pillars rose into the air. They were covered with gold. Military officers, priests, and important government officials in fancy court dress packed the room.

"He is coming! He is here!"

The king entered alone. He strode into the hall with slow measured steps. He did not look to the right or left. A gold-sheathed sword hung at his side. His clothes were covered with gold.

Although he knew that God was in control of all things, Adoniram trembled. He had never seen a real king before!

The king stopped just in front of him. He looked down at the foreign men. Adoniram looked up and met the king's eyes.

"Who are these men?" the king inquired.

"We are teachers, great king," Adoniram replied in Burmese.

"You speak the Burmese tongue," His Majesty said. "How is it that you speak our language so well? When did you arrive? Are you teachers of religion? Are you married? Why do you dress so strangely?"

Adoniram was astonished by all the questions, but he answered them plainly and clearly in Burmese.

"Ah," said the king. He moved off to the throne, rested his hand on the hilt of his golden sword, and fixed his eyes on Adoniram.

"We are from the country of America," Adoniram said. "We are explainers of the Christian religion. We want to present this religion to the people of Burma, so they will enjoy heaven forever. May we please have permission from the king to preach Christianity freely in your great country?"

The king reached out to take one of Adoniram's tracts from a court official. He began to read it over to himself.

Adoniram's heart pounded hard. If the king read the news that there was a God in heaven and wanted to hear more, all would be well. But if not—

"No," said the king, dashing the tract to the ground.

Adoniram could hardly breathe. Tears trickled out of his eyes and ran down his cheeks. He looked at Dr. Price, but Dr. Price did not look back. His face, too, was crushed under sorrow.

There was one last hope.

"We have brought you a marvelous gift, your majesty," Adoniram said, "We bring our Holy Book to you." He held out the gold-covered Bible to the king. Perhaps the king would want to touch the gold at least or look at the English words on the pages.

"No," the king said again, waving the Bible away. Adoniram sank down to his knees beside Dr. Price. The king rose from his throne and strode away to the other end of the hall. He threw himself down on a richly covered cushion and gazed out at the people below.

"You must go now," the court official whispered to Adoniram.

Adoniram and Dr. Price rose quickly and left the hall. They heard the quiet snickering of the Burmese priests who did not want them to preach the gospel. "Now no one will listen to you," one of the priests said. "They will hear what the king has done, and they, too, will refuse to read the books you bring."

Adoniram and Dr. Price walked quickly out to the streets of Ava. Dust swirled around them, and the hot sun glared down on them as they walked away from the palace.

The journey back home to Rangoon was filled with sorrow. All they could think of was the look on the king's face when he had rejected the first knowledge he had ever had of the One True God.

As their boat skimmed over the Irrawaddy River, Adoniram's thoughts turned to home. "It will be good to see Ann again," he said, "and the other believers, and the new missionaries."

"And Moung Shwa-gnong!" said Dr. Price. "Look, Adoniram, there he is, on the bank of the river!"

Adoniram looked up. It was true! Moung Shwa-gnong was waving hard from the edge of the river.

"Teacher! Teacher!" he called above the sound of the water that slapped against the side of the boat. "I have become a Christian! I have trusted the Savior!"

Adoniram sat back in the boat and smiled. He looked at Dr. Price and laughed out loud. "Now here is something wonderful," he said. "The king of Burma has turned his back on God, but God has not turned his back on the people of Burma."

Dr. Price reached out and shook Adoniram's hand. "There are many souls to be saved in this city. I think we should get back to work."

"You are right," Adoniram said. "There is no time to waste."

11
English Spies

"I want to move to Ava," Adoniram said. He and Ann were walking through the marketplace in Rangoon.

Ann said nothing. She stared straight ahead as they walked.

"Please say something, Ann," Adoniram said.

"All right," she said quietly. "I'll say this: I don't think we should go to Ava. You are needed here. The Rangoon church is growing. Even Moung Shwa-gnong has been baptized. The last time you went to Ava, the king did not look on you with favor. It could be very dangerous for us."

Adoniram placed some fresh-caught fish in the basket. He thanked the fishseller and paid

him. "I believe God wants us to go there," he said quietly.

"Then we will go," Ann said. "But what about our group of believers here?"

"Other missionaries are here now," Adoniram said. "There are eighteen Burmese Christians and many more who are beginning to seek after Jesus. I am sure they will be fine. If we stay here, perhaps no one will ever go back to Ava."

"I'm ready to go wherever you go," Ann said.

Over the next few days, Ann worked hard packing all their things. Adoniram hurried around, talking to the Burmese Christians, giving last minute instructions and advice to the other missionaries, and finally, gathering for a final prayer session with the little church before they left.

"We're all ready, Adoniram," Ann said. "The boat is packed—especially the work you have done on the New Testament."

"Off to Ava then," Adoniram said.

They stood in the boat and waved at the white missionaries and the brown Burmese Christians, standing together for Christ, waving good-bye.

As they traveled up the river, Ann and Adoniram passed many villages. Sometimes they got out and walked through the streets and talked to the people about Christ.

At one village, a man ran over to the crowd that had gathered around them. "May I have a writing about this new religion?" the man asked.

"Of course you may," Adoniram said. He handed the man one of the Christian tracts he had written in Burmese. The man moved off under a tree to read it. After a little while, he came back.

"This tract is good," the teacher said. "Please allow me to copy it so that I may study it further."

"You may keep it," Adoniram said, "if you promise to read it to all your neighbors."

"I will read it to everyone," the man said.

That night back on the boat, Ann and Adoniram prayed for the people of this village.

Finally they arrived at their new home in Ava. Right away, Adoniram began to preach the gospel every day.

"Things are going so well," Adoniram said one day. "The king's officials do not give us any trouble, and many people want to know about Christianity."

"Yes," Ann said. "Let us pray we can continue serving God here in Ava for a long time. We will have a new baby in just a few weeks, and I will be glad to stay here for the rest of my life!"

Just then there was a loud knock on the bamboo door. A man burst into the house. Adoniram stood up. "What is it, friend?" he said.

"War!" the man said. "War has been declared between Burma and England! You must leave at once or you will be killed!"

"We are Americans," Adoniram said. "We are not English. There is no reason we should be harmed."

"Many people think you are English spies," the man said. "Please, leave this city now."

After the man left, Adoniram turned to Ann. She was trembling all over.

"I am so frightened, Adoniram," she said. "I do not know if we can convince these people that we are not English. After all, we look the same, and we speak the same language."

"I am frightened too," he said. "Let's ask God what we should do."

Suddenly there was a great crash as the bamboo door was smashed apart. Men with sticks and whips charged into the house. Ann screamed.

"Who are you?" Adoniram shouted. "What are you doing?"

Ann backed into a corner, and Adoniram stood in front of her.

"Where is the foreign teacher?" a man yelled.

"I am here," Adoniram said.

"You are an English spy," they said. "We are arresting you!"

"No," Ann screamed. "We are Americans! We are not English."

The men did not listen. They threw Adoniram to the floor and tied his legs together. Then they dragged him out of the house and through the city streets. They arrived at a fenced enclosure. Inside the fence was a low building with no windows. A fierce-looking man stood at the door to the building. When he saw Adoniram, he opened the door wide.

"Get in there," he said, and the other men kicked Adoniram inside.

Adoniram squinted his eyes, but still could see nothing. The place stank. When his eyes became accustomed to the pale light, he saw that there were more than one hundred prisoners in the room. There were no windows.

Adoniram was knocked to the ground. Iron shackles were put around his legs, binding him so that he could not walk or even stand. He lay back onto the filthy floor. Soon he felt something crawling on his leg. He slapped at it with his tied-up hands. A large bug squished under his fingers.

Adoniram prayed for help in this dismal jail. He prayed for Ann and for the baby she was expecting. He prayed for the Burmese who had begun learning about the Lord Jesus Christ.

Even in prison he preached to the other inmates. Most of them were criminals who had robbed and killed people. Adoniram knew they might get angry with him, but still he told them about Jesus.

"After all," he thought. "They are tied up like I am, and they can't hurt me!"

Soon more white missionaries were thrown into the jail.

"John Price," Adoniram said. "I am glad to see you, though I wish it would have been somewhere else."

"They think we are all spies for England," Dr. Price said. "We will be forgotten in this hole."

"God has not forgotten us," Adoniram said. "We are His children, and He still has work for us here in Burma."

"We'll see if you still think that in a few more days!" the guard said. Then he ran a cord through the prisoners' leg shackles and hoisted it over a ceiling beam. All the prisoners' legs were now suspended in the air. Only their shoulders and heads lay on the ground.

"Happy dreams," the guard called.

Soon Adoniram's whole body ached. "Dear God," he prayed. "Give us strength to bear this suffering."

The next day, the guard entered the dark prison room. He walked straight to Adoniram. Adoniram trembled with fear.

"You have a visitor," the guard said. He dragged Adoniram outside of the prison building.

"Ann!" Adoniram said. "What are you doing here? Go home. This is no place for you."

"I brought you some food," she said. "I love you, and I will come to see you as often as I can."

A few weeks later, Ann gave birth to baby Maria. When she felt well enough, she brought the baby with her to visit Adoniram again.

"Thank you for bringing her, Ann," Adoniram said. "Seeing her sweet baby face makes me so happy."

Adoniram grew thin and weak in the prison. His clothes wore out and began to fall apart. He became ill, and his body was covered with sores.

"I think I will die here, Ann," he said one day. "Take care of yourself and the baby. Do not worry about me any more."

For a while Ann did not come. Adoniram knew he had told her not to come, but he very much wanted to see her.

"Your wife cannot come anymore, Prisoner Judson," the guard said one day. "I have heard that she has smallpox. She might die." He laughed at Adoniram and stomped away.

Adoniram worried. If Ann had smallpox, she would be unable to care for baby Maria. And if Maria too caught this terrible disease, she might die.

"Please heal Ann," he prayed. "And please, dear Lord, let Maria live."

Days passed. Then, one hot afternoon, the guard came in, unlocked Adoniram's iron shackles and hauled him outside.

"You have visitors," he said, throwing Adoniram to the ground.

"Ann! Maria!" Adoniram struggled to get up. "You are well, thank the Lord."

"I cannot stay long," she said. "But I wanted to see you." She reached into her satchel. "I brought you a little food and some medicine for your sores."

Adoniram loved these visits. He loved seeing baby Maria. He loved seeing the smile on Ann's face.

"It gives me strength to live knowing that you will come to see me."

Adoniram began to feel a little happier, though the prison was just as filthy and the food was just as bad. Then one day the guard came into the main prison room. "Everybody get up," he shouted. "We are leaving this wretched place."

"Good," the prisoners said.

"Ha, ha," said the guard. "We are going to a place that is even worse!"

17
Oung-Pen-La

"Hurry up, you slow pokes," the guard said. He cracked his long leather whip hard, flicking the back of a prisoner, drawing blood. "Go faster, faster!"

It took hours to walk to the new prison. All the prisoners were chained together. When one tripped and fell, others were pulled down with him.

Adoniram's shoes had rotted away a long time ago. He stumbled over the rocks in the path until his feet bled. The sun beat down on his head and neck and back. He longed for new clothes, for a bath, for good food, for a day without pain.

"Welcome to the Oung-pen-la prison," said the jailer. "Now get inside."

Adoniram found a place to lie down inside the building. His feet were bleeding. His stomach churned with hunger, and his throat ached with thirst. He looked up and noticed that there was no roof on the building.

When it began to rain, he was drenched. He shivered with fever in the night. Insects crawled through the warm wet clothing.

"There is one good thing," Adoniram thought as he killed a cockroach. "Ann will not be able to visit me here. She will stay at home in Ava and take care of Maria. Then if I live through this ordeal, she will be healthy enough to look after me."

However, the next day, Ann and Maria arrived at Oung-pen-la.

"What are you doing here?" Adoniram said. "You should not have come here."

"I go where you go," she said. "I will share in your sufferings."

"Go home," Adoniram said. "I am going to die soon. You cannot help me anymore."

Ann smiled gently up at Adoniram. "I shall stay with you here," she said. "I have not traveled across the world with you in order to leave you now."

Six months passed. Ann visited Adoniram during the day. She and Maria cuddled together on a cot in a tiny room outside the prison fence at night.

"I am out of medicine," Ann told Adoniram one day. "I must go back to Ava and get some. I will be back in a few days."

Three days passed. Ann did not return. Many more days passed.

"Maybe she has decided to stay in Ava," Adoniram thought.

"A passing merchant told me that your wife is very ill," the prison guard told him. "People are gathered around your house in Ava waiting for her to die."

Adoniram could not believe it. What would happen to Maria if Ann died? What would happen to him?

Weeks passed.

"Your wife came back last night," the guard told Adoniram.

"Can I see her?" he said. "Where is she?"

"She is dying again," he said. "Come, I will show you."

The guard took Adoniram to the little room where Ann was. She had collapsed on a cot and could not move. Adoniram felt her forehead.

"She is burning up!" he said.

"That is not my concern. Why don't you pray to that God of yours to help her?"

Adoniram prayed. He picked up his helpless baby daughter. "Maria has no food," he said to the guard. "Please, may I find a woman in the village to feed her?"

The man looked at the tiny sick baby and laughed. "I don't care. Do what you wish with her. She is going to die anyway."

Adoniram left Ann tossing with fever and trudged through the village of Oung-pen-la. He cradled little Maria in his arms. When people saw him approaching, they ran into their houses and slammed the bamboo doors. He realized he must look frightening—he was so thin, and sores from the shackles and insect bites scarred his body. He was unwashed, and he was bright red from the burning heat of the sun that shone on the roofless prison day after day.

"Please," he called out. "My baby needs milk. She will die without milk. Someone have mercy. Please have pity on baby Maria."

Adoniram sat down on a tree stump in the middle of the village. All around him were the shut doors of bamboo houses, thatched with dried grass. He longed for the cool rolling hills of New England, the abundant food and milk of America. The medicine, the peace, the freedom of his homeland.

"I will help her, sir."

Adoniram looked up. A young Burmese woman stood beside him. She looked strong and healthy.

Adoniram breathed deeply. He kissed the top of Maria's head and wept over her. Then he held her out to the stranger. "Thank you," he said. "You have saved her life. When her mother is well, she will come to get her."

The young woman nodded. "I too am a mother," she said. "I will do this for her mother and for you." The woman's eyes were soft. She smiled. "The war is hard," she said. "It is hard for everyone, but it will be over soon."

Adoniram hobbled back to the prison. His feet still bled. The leg irons still gouged into his flesh, leaving deep wounds. He collapsed onto his thin bed of straw. A man beside him began to laugh.

"Why are you laughing?" Adoniram asked. "What is there to laugh about?"

"I am laughing at you," the man said. "I think you are crazy. Now, look at me." Adoniram looked. The man was tall and bony. He had scars all over his body and several of his teeth were gone.

"I am in prison because I am a murderer and a thief. You are in prison because you won't go home to America where you belong. I have heard that it is easy to live in America. You did not go home to peace and safety when the war started. Now you are in a death prison, your wife is dying, and you have given your baby to a woman you don't even know. You see, you are crazy."

"He's not crazy," another prisoner said. "He's stupid. He serves a God who has forsaken him!"

"I am not crazy," said Adoniram. "And I am not stupid. I know that every one of these trials has been planned by God to make me more like Jesus Christ."

The men talked on into the night. Many said, "He is crazy," and others said, "No, he is a good man." Finally, the talk died down as the men drifted off to sleep.

Suddenly, there was a great noise outside the prison walls. There were loud shouts and beating drums.

"What is it?" Adoniram asked. "What is happening?"

The prison door slammed open and the guard entered the roofless room. He walked past the murderers and the thieves. He stopped in front of the missionaries.

"Good news at last," the guard said, leering at them. "The war is over. You are free to go home."

"Go to America," the murderer called to Adoniram. "It is an easy life there."

"I go to get my wife and baby," Adoniram said. "And then I go back to Rangoon to preach the gospel of Jesus Christ."

13 Hopia Tree Sorrows

"I have never felt so free," Adoniram said. He tilted his head back and looked up into the clear blue sky. The yellow sun shone brightly on the Irrawaddy River, making it shimmer like polished silver. The wind swirled about their faces and through their hair. Adoniram held baby Maria in his arms. Ann stood at his side. They were weak. They were exhausted. But they were free!

When at last the boat docked in Rangoon, Adoniram and Ann looked out over the familiar city and smiled. God had brought them home.

"Let us get back to the mission quickly!" Adoniram said. "I'm so excited to see how many people have been saved since we moved to Ava."

They rushed through the streets of Rangoon, but saw no one they knew. As soon as they caught sight of the mission house, they hurried toward it, Adoniram running ahead.

"Hello!" he called. There was no answer.

"Maybe they are in the yard around back," Ann said.

Ann and Adoniram ran through the mission yard. There was no one there.

"Maybe they are in the zayat praying," Adoniram said. He ran off down the road, but returned a few minutes later, his head bowed.

"It's deserted, Ann," he said. "Even the door is missing. Do you think all the Christians have gone back to serving idols?"

"It can't be," Ann said. "If they have all gone away, then we will have nothing to show for all our years here except for the scars of your imprisonment." Ann sat down on the ground and wept. "This is too hard," she said.

They sat alone in the house that night. Maria had been put to bed, and now there was nothing to say. If all the disciples had gone away, they would have to start over from the beginning.

Just then there was a light tap on the window. It was Moung Nau!

"We are still here," Moung Nau said. "It has been hard to stand for Christ without you, but now that you are back, things will be better. I am sorry we were not stronger."

Adoniram and Moung Nau talked late into the night. Adoniram told Moung Nau about the prisons in Ava and Oung-pen-la. Moung Nau told Adoniram how the English had taken over Rangoon during the war.

"We suffered much," he said. "Soldiers roamed the streets. Thieves ran through the town and stole everything. Buildings were destroyed. Many people died. And now there is a famine here. There is not enough food for the wild beasts in the jungle. Tigers are coming into the city for food! They carry off the cattle. Even some people have been killed by tigers."

"Stay inside," Adoniram told Ann the next morning. "Don't let Maria out of your sight."

Adoniram began to preach in the zayat every day. Few people came. Most people spent all day trying to find enough food. Sometimes a hungry tiger would walk right down the street looking for something to eat!

"We cannot stay here," Adoniram said at last. "It is too dangerous."

"Where will we go?" Ann asked.

"We shall move to Amherst," Adoniram said. "It is also in Burma, but the English army is there, so we will have freedom to preach the gospel."

"Are there tigers there too?" Ann said. She clutched baby Maria to her.

"I think there are tigers there too," he said, "but they stay in the jungle!"

The small town of Amherst sat on the edge of the sea. Adoniram began to preach in Burmese every day. Many Burmese people came to hear the word of God, and many believed on the Lord Jesus Christ.

One night Adoniram came to the dinner table with a strange look on his face.

"Why are you so sad?" Ann said. "You were right about moving to Amherst. You can freely preach the gospel every day. Moung Nau and the other disciples like it here, and many people are being saved. The New Testament is almost completed and soon there will be one hundred disciples. We are all healthy. You should be happy, not sad. Here, sit down and have some dinner."

Adoniram did not speak. He moved toward Ann and held out a letter in his hand. Ann wiped her hands on her apron and sat down in a chair to read the letter.

"Oh, no," she said. "They want you to go to Ava to translate for the government. You will have to see the king again!"

"I don't want to go back to Ava, Ann," he said. "The king's rejection, the prison, the terrible diseases we had there—they are all so fresh in my memory, and so painful. Thinking of Ava makes me wish I had never left America. Think of the wonderful family we could have had there!"

Ann looked deeply into Adoniram's face. "If we had stayed in America, there would be no Burmese Christians. Go to Ava and do the work of God."

Adoniram sighed. "You are right. Perhaps this will be the time God will open the king's heart to listen to the gospel."

Adoniram left Ann with a heavy heart. He kissed her and little Maria and once again boarded a boat. The boat took him across the bay to Rangoon and then up the Irrawaddy River to Ava.

As Adoniram passed the familiar sights of the Irrawaddy River, he remembered the wretched time he had spent in the prisons at Ava and Oung-pen-la, and the joyful feeling of freedom when he had been released at last.

"Perhaps this will be the best trip to Ava of all," he said.

When his interpreting work was done, Adoniram once again approached the king for permission to spread the gospel throughout Burma.

"No," the king said again.

Adoniram was heartbroken. He wandered back to the room at the inn and lay down on the bed. "I have come all the way up here for nothing." he said. He jumped up and began to throw his things into his traveling bag. "I will go home immediately. Ann and Maria and I will live in Amherst and be happy."

Just then there was a knock on the door. "Who is it?" Adoniram called.

A Burmese man entered the room and handed a letter to Adoniram.

"Thank you," Adoniram said. "I'm always glad to get letters from home!" Then he saw that the envelope was bordered in black, he sat down on the bed. A black border meant that someone close to him had died. His hands shook as he opened the envelope.

He wondered if it was his father or mother back in America who had died, and this thought made him very sad.

Then he read the letter. "Dear Sir," the letter said. "I am sorry to bring you these sad tidings. Your beloved wife Ann is dead."

Adoniram took the next boat back to Amherst. The other missionaries met his boat. He took Maria into his arms and gently kissed her.

Together with Maria, he picked some wild flowers to place on Ann's grave. The grave lay beneath a hopia tree.

"All I ever gave you was poverty, heartache, and tears," he said. "I wanted to give you so much more."

"Mama in heaven," Maria said. Adoniram nodded and took his little girl in his arms. "Yes," he said. "Mama in heaven."

Six months later, Maria died. She was two years old.

"I will bury her under the hopia tree by her mother," Adoniram said. His voice was flat, his face white and drawn. For days he sat in a chair by the window that looked out into the harsh Burmese jungle. He would not eat, and he

drank little. Friends came to visit, but none could comfort him. "I am drinking the cup of sorrow to the very bottom," he said. "It is a very bitter cup."

One night he stared at his bamboo wall for several hours, hardly thinking, only grieving. At last he stood up and walked out onto the bamboo deck. He thought of little Maria. She had been so small and frail. He thought of Ann. Her sweet smiling face filled his mind, and he remembered what she liked to tell him when times were hard: "The future is as bright as all the promises of God."

Tears ran down Adoniram's face. "God will yet have a Christian church in Burma," he said. "And the Bible will be translated into Burmese. God has many people here to save." He struggled to his feet. "I will get back to work."

14 Karen Jungles

The old lady coughed into her lace-gloved hand. "Well," she said. "Is this the way the famous American missionary lives?" She stared around Adoniram's simple house.

"Yes," Adoniram said. "I live alone here in the jungle." He smiled. "Though I'm not really alone, you know. Insects and rodents keep me company day and night."

The lady shuddered. "What sort of adventures do you have?"

"I preach the gospel and translate the word of God. The New Testament is finished and the Old Testament is coming along nicely. We have over one hundred believers in our church."

"That's not the sort of adventure I was referring to," the English lady said. "What I mean is—oh, no! What is that? It's a bat! Help! Help!"

Adoniram smiled, but jumped to his feet to wave the bat away from the English lady's head.

"Yes, we have bats in our houses," he said. "I hardly notice them anymore. I suppose I have gotten used to them."

"Well, then, why didn't you tell me that?" the lady said. "That is just the sort of adventure I wish to write about you when I get back home."

"Ah," said Adoniram softly. "But it is not what I wish you to write about me. I wish you to write that we are here preaching the gospel and seeing immortal souls turn to Jesus Christ."

The English lady waved her fan frantically at a bat. It settled on her hat for a second, but flew off when she screamed. "You are a great man, Mr. Judson," she said. "But this is truly a dreadful place. You have been here for many years. Surely you have done enough for God in Burma. Have you ever thought about going home to America?"

"Yes," Adoniram said. "I think about it often. Every time I see a ship leaving port, I think that if I were on it, I would be home with my family in just a few months."

"Then why ever do you stay here?" the lady asked. "You could preach the gospel in America as easily as you do here."

"There are thousands of men who can preach in English, ma'am," he said. "But there are only five or six people in the whole world who can preach the gospel in Burmese. If I go home to America, who will do God's work here?"

In the distance a tiger roared. The English lady trembled at the sound. She swatted at a few more bats, stomped on a trail of ants, and kicked a cockroach out of her way as she backed down the ladder to the ground. "Good-bye, Mr. Judson," she said.

"Good-bye," he said. After he saw that she had run safely back to the main mission house, he burst into laughter. He laughed and laughed. "A bat on her hat!" he said. "That should be enough of an adventure for her whole lifetime!"

The next morning, Adoniram gathered ten Burmese believers around him. "Gentlemen," he said. "An English lady wondered if we have adventures. I have a wonderful adventure in mind. Who will go with me?"

The men nodded. "We will all go, Teacher. You have brought us the truth of Jesus Christ. For you we will do anything."

"Then pack a few things you will need. We are going deep into the jungle." He shielded his eyes from the bright morning sun and looked off toward the dense jungle. Trailing vines lined the path, and trees rose up high as if to block their way. "In there, my friends, is great adventure," he said. "We will work our way into the jungle and find people who have never heard the gospel. We will tell them the greatest truth in all the world."

Adoniram and his men hunched their packs onto their backs. They carried strong walking sticks to help them over the rocky paths, through the tangled jungle creepers, over stony streams, and through deep, rushing rivers.

They climbed high mountains. They scrambled into trees when wild beasts came lumbering down the paths. At night they slept outside under the midnight stars with only their mosquito netting to keep the thousands of tiny insects from buzzing around their faces and in their ears all night long.

One evening, as the other men slept, Adoniram gazed up at the full moon that shone through the tall leafy trees. A great sorrow filled his heart as he thought of his wife, Ann, and their baby, Maria, who were buried at Amherst under the hopia tree.

He wondered about his family that remained in America. He knew he would probably never see them again. Never see his parents or Abigail or Elnathan again! Never see the rolling hills of New England or the orange, red, and purple leaves of the brilliant New England autumn.

The sorrow of his heart overwhelmed him, and he began to cry.

"Teacher," a man said softly. "Are you sad?"

"Sometimes I feel so alone." Adoniram said.

"You are not alone, dear Teacher," the man said. "The God who put these great mountains and great forests here, this same God loves you, Teacher. This same God sent you across the ocean to tell us of His Son, Jesus Christ."

"Thank you, my friend, for reminding me," Adoniram said.

He spent the rest of the night thinking about what the man had said—*This same God*. In the morning, he realized there was still much work to be done.

"This same God has scattered immortal souls through this jungle, my friends," he said. "Let us go out into the jungle and find them and tell them of the God who made them."

For days they slogged through fallen branches and twisted vines. The screech of monkeys and the trumpeting of elephants filled the air. They sloshed their way through streams. Their shoes wore out, and they continued barefooted. They climbed mountains.

"This adventure seems impossible sometimes, Teacher," a man said.

Adoniram smiled. The other men also smiled. They knew what the Teacher would say: "With God nothing is impossible."

One morning they arrived at a Karen village. The Karen people did not live in great cities. They lived in villages scattered through the Burmese jungle. They were very poor and spent their days gathering food to eat.

"Most Burmese look down on the Karen people," a disciple said. "They call them wild men and are afraid of them."

"I, too, am afraid of the Karens," another man said. "I have heard that they are great sinners."

"We are all sinners," Adoniram said. "Let us tell these Karens about Jesus."

That afternoon a group of Karens assembled around them. Some sat on mats made of leaves. Others sat on the bare ground. Looking around the group of raggedly-dressed people, Adoniram could not help but think of the well-clothed people he had seen on his visit to Ava, especially the great king in his golden robes!

Suddenly, a tall dignified man came out of a small hut. He was dressed in a splendid robe.

"I am the chief of this village," the man said. "And I am also a sorcerer!" He waved a wand. The Karen people cringed in fear, but Adoniram and the other Christians did not tremble. The man walked up to Adoniram and looked at him closely. "You have a white face," he said.

"Yes," said Adoniram. "I come from a land far away where many people have faces like mine."

The sorcerer turned to the assembled people. "He has a white face!" the man shouted. Then he turned back to Adoniram and bowed before him. "We have a legend," he said, "that a white man will someday come to us from far across the ocean to tell us the way to heaven. Are you that man?"

Adoniram was astonished! He cleared his throat. "Yes," he said. "I am that man. I have come to tell you about the Savior of the world, Jesus Christ."

"Aha," said the sorcerer. "We will all listen to you. Tell us about this Savior."

For the rest of the day, Adoniram told the Karen people about the Lord Jesus Christ, about His death on the cross, how He had been raised from the dead, and how all those who forsake their sins and trust in Him will live with God forever in heaven.

"This is what we have been needing to hear," the chief said. "I wish to know this Savior. I wish to follow Him. I shall dress in my most elegant robes every day to show that I honor Him."

"Your nice clothes do not impress the Lord Jesus Christ," Adoniram said. "In fact, if those are the robes of a sorcerer, then you must discard them or you will not be following Christ."

"What?" the man said. "Do you mean to say that God is not impressed when I dress so fine?"

"He is not," said Adoniram. "And He will not accept you if you cling to your sorcery."

The man looked around at the villagers. Then he looked back at Adoniram.

"In that case, I shall never wear it again," he said. He took off his fancy robe and began tearing it into thin strips. "If Christ is not pleased with this robe, I shall throw it into that stream there and never see it again!" At this moment he handed his wand to Adoniram. "Take it," he said. "Break it in pieces. I follow only Jesus Christ now."

"You see," Adoniram said, as he gathered his disciples around him that night. "God has people everywhere. Even when I am gone from you, you must keep looking for the people who will be saved."

"Are you leaving us, Teacher?" a man said.

"I have no plans to leave you," Adoniram said. "But some day I will die. I cannot live forever on the earth, can I?" He looked around at the men. "And when that day comes, I hope you will continue to press on further into the jungle, further into Burma, and even further to Siam and China. Tell more and more people about Christ. Tell your children and your grandchildren."

The disciples looked back at their teacher and nodded. "We will tell everyone about Jesus," they said.

Afterword

In spite of sorrow, loss, and pain
Our course be onward still.
We sow in Burma's barren plain
We reap on Zion's hill.

—Adoniram Judson

When Adoniram Judson arrived in Burma in 1813, there was not a single Burmese Christian. By the time of his death in 1850, he had translated the entire Bible into Burmese, and more than seven thousand Burmese people had trusted in Jesus Christ for salvation.

Today there are about one-and-a-half million Christians in Burma (Myanmar). There is a Baptist church in the village of Oung-pen-la.

Eighty-seven percent of the people of Burma are Buddhists. The Shway Dagon pagoda still stands in Rangoon.

The future is as bright as
the promises of God.